Trinkets

For Isobel and Maureen,
two of the most creative
and inspiring people I have
the honour to know.

Cat
Rabbit

Trinkets

Smith
Street
Books

Contents

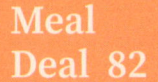

Hi! My name is **Cat Rabbit.** I have been making felt trinkets for many years. I like to make them as gifts for friends, decorations for special occasions and just to make me smile in my everyday life. They only require a small handful of materials — often things you can find around the house — and just a few hours of your time, once you learn the steps. Let me show you!

WHAT YOU WILL NEED

Tracing paper for your template pieces

A pencil for tracing your template pieces, and for stuffing hard-to-reach places

PVA glue

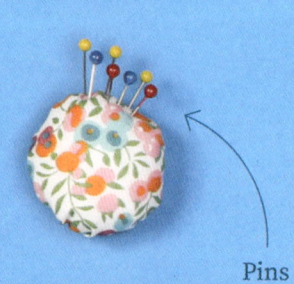

Pins

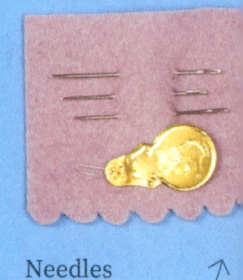

Needles and needle threader

Waxed string, ribbon or sturdy yarn

Small, sharp scissors

Plastic eyes and washers
(see page 16 for alternatives)

Felt in
lots of
colours

*You can also use
old, felted, woollen
jumpers and
blankets!*

Thread
in lots of
colours

Stuffing
(or the inside
of an old obliging
cushion insert)

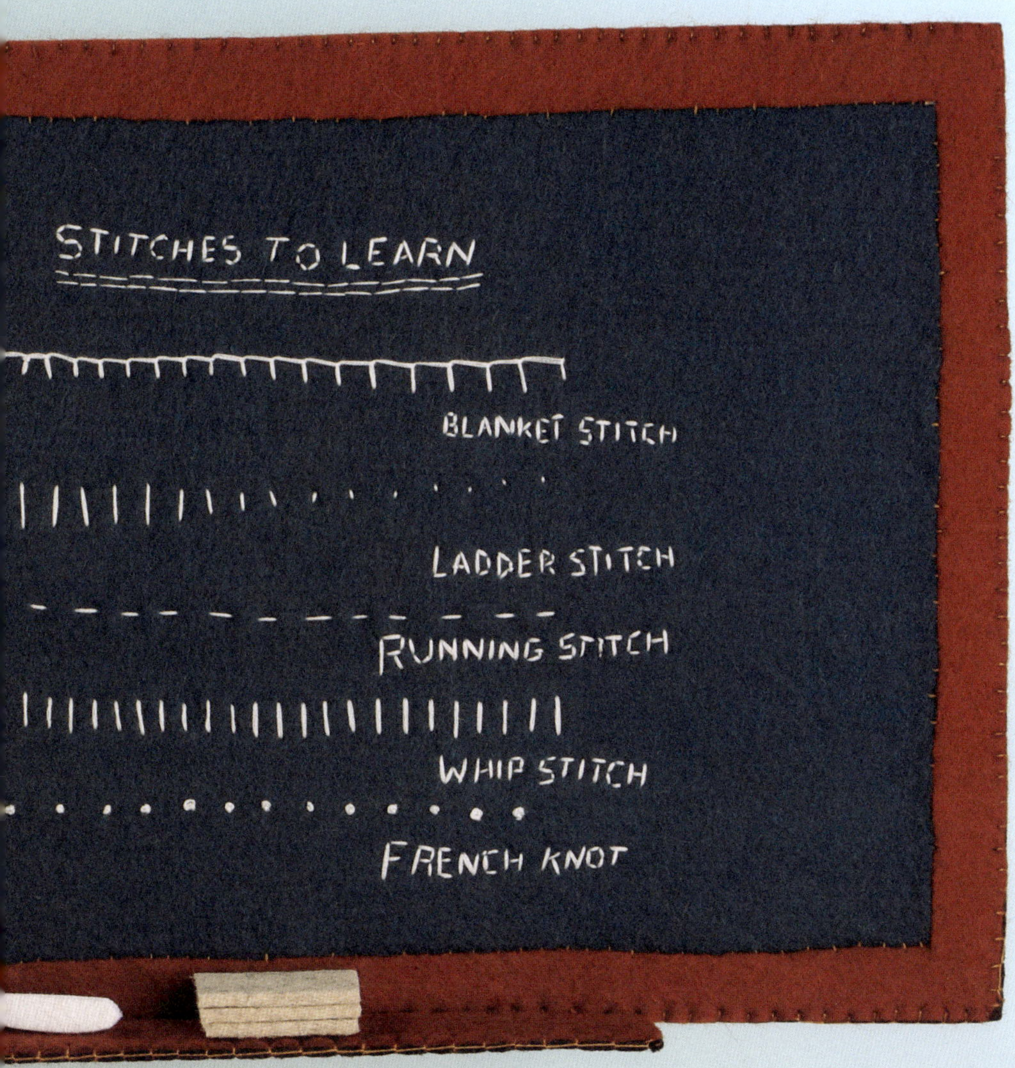

STITCHES TO LEARN

BLANKET STITCH

LADDER STITCH

RUNNING STITCH

WHIP STITCH

FRENCH KNOT

Blanket stitch: This is a very useful stitch! It creates a decorative, rounded edge, and has the practical purpose of preventing any stuffing from popping out.

Pass your needle through the felt, pausing halfway to loop the thread underneath the tip of the needle before pulling it all the way through.

Ladder stitch: This stitch is very handy for invisibly closing seams from the outside of your trinket. Starting on the wrong side of the seam closest to you, poke your needle up through the felt, then pass the thread over the open seam and through the felt on the other side. Poke the needle back up on the same side to begin your next stitch. Continue back and forth in this fashion, forming stitches akin to the rungs of a ladder. Gently pull your thread every few stitches to close the seam.

The 'wrong side' is the side of your felt that won't be on display.

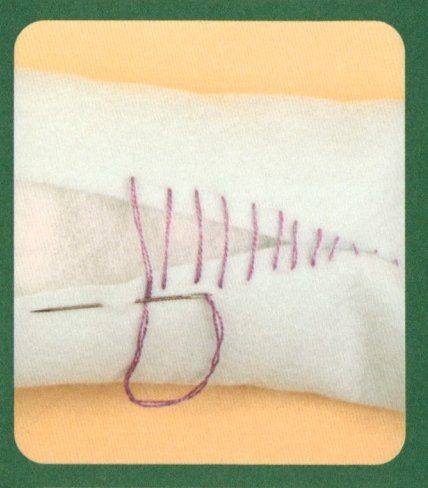

Running stitch: This stitch allows you to gather your felt when the thread is pulled.

Pass your needle in and out of the felt at regular intervals. If required, gather the felt by pulling the thread. To secure, sew a few tiny stitches into the wrong side of your trinket, to keep the gathered material in place.

Whip stitch: Use this stitch to attach (or appliqué) one piece of felt on top of another.

Pin your felt pieces in place. Starting underneath, poke your needle up through the top layer of felt, then pass your thread over the edge and poke your needle through to the underside of the bottom layer.

For a diagonal effect, pass the thread over the edge at an angle.

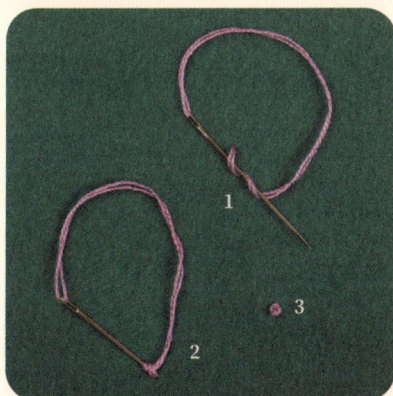

French knot: A decorative stitch for adding unique touches, such as pickle lumps and orange bumps, or facial features such as round eyes and pinchable cheeks.

Pull your needle through to the front of your felt and wind the thread around the needle one or two times (the more times you wind, the bulkier your knot will be). Poke the needle back through the felt at the point where it came out and pull tight.

Tie off your thread: When you come to the end of a seam or are running out of thread, sew five or six tiny stitches in the same place, into the wrong side of your project (or, if this isn't possible, 'stitch in the ditch', i.e., through the channel of a seam), before snipping your thread. This will anchor your stitches and prevent all your hard work from unravelling.

Freestyle stitch: There are a couple of moments in this book where I tell you to freestyle! This is where you can let loose and follow your heart. Or think of it as slow, steady drawing using thread. And, like drawing, you can erase or unpick at any time and start afresh.

Faces

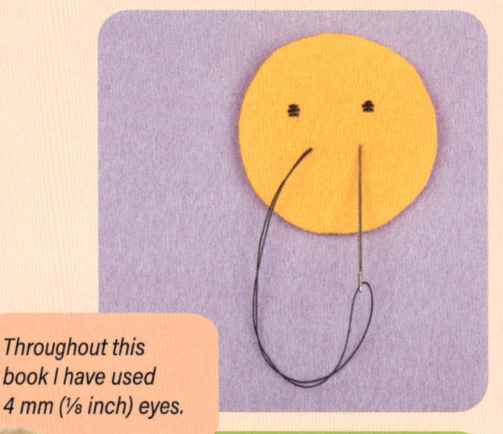

Many of the faces in this book are simply created with a few straight stitches. A straight stitch is just as it sounds: bring your needle and thread up through your felt at the beginning of the stitch, and pull them back down through the felt at the end of the stitch.

Throughout this book I have used 4 mm (⅛ inch) eyes.

Some of the patterns in this book call for plastic eyes. These eyes come with small metal or plastic washers and are available from craft stores in many sizes. To affix this style of eye, make a small incision in the felt with the sharp point of your scissors, pass the stalk of the eye through the hole, then press the washer firmly onto the stalk on the wrong side of the felt.

If you can't find plastic eyes (or don't want to buy new things/ leave your house), there are many alternatives: beads, sequins, fabric markers and paint, googly eyes, buttons and even scrap felt cut into tiny features and glued on. Have a rummage through your craft supplies and use your imagination!

A pleasant, open-eyed face is my go-to. For the first eye, stitch a group of three small, straight stitches on top of each other, then move the thread to where you'd like the other eye to be and repeat. One straight stitch forms the mouth.

You might like to add emotions to your trinkets. Three straight stitches curved upwards make a very happy felt friend; add eyebrows and it's also surprised! If you'd like to further embellish your trinket, stitch some tiny cheeks, freckles or even eyelashes.

The face is where you get to add your own little splash of pizazz, and, in my opinion, a wonky face is a good face. I have built my entire sewing practice on wonkiness, so my advice is don't get caught up in perfection! A handmade trinket is a unique treasure that can't be repeated.

RECIPES

Throughout this book I have used 18 cm (7 inch) lengths of waxed string to create the looped strings on each trinket. You could also use ribbon or yarn.

Some of the trinkets in this book require a knotted string. To knot your trinket string, fold it in half and pinch the two ends in your non-dominant hand and the folded point in your other. Create a loop and pull the folded point through, while using your hand to shift the knot as close to the ends of the string as possible, before pulling tight.

Nibble Platter

Stitch up an impressive tasting board of your favourite fluffy snacks!

Cracker Stack

Lucky Pickle

Baby Mayo

BFF Cheeses

LUCKY PICKLE

Who doesn't need a good-luck pickle in their pocket?
The Lucky Pickle works equally well at keeping your keys safe
or dangling happily from your backpack.

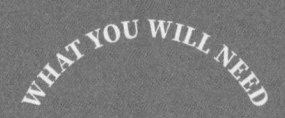

WHAT YOU WILL NEED

- ◯ Tracing paper
- ◯ Pencil
- ◯ Scissors
- ◯ Green felt
- ◯ Plastic eyes and washers
- ◯ Needle
- ◯ Black thread
- ◯ Pink thread
- ◯ Pins
- ◯ Green thread
- ◯ Waxed string
- ◯ A handful of stuffing

Trace and cut your Lucky Pickle pieces from the template (page 132).

Take one pickle piece and use scissors to help insert the eyes and fasten with the washers (page 16), about a quarter of the way down. Use black thread to stitch a mouth, then use pink thread to stitch some rosy freckles.

Lay another pickle piece on top of the face, making sure the face is on the inside and the contours of the pickle pieces are aligned. Using green thread and blanket stitch (page 12), start at the top and sew one seam of the pickle pieces together.

Add the third pickle piece, and sew up the second seam from the base, leaving a small gap at the top where the pieces meet. For this seam, you may need to manipulate the felt pieces a little so that the inward curve of one piece hugs the outward curve of the other.

Set your pickle aside for a small moment.

Curving the felt is a little tricky, but it's what gives your pickle friend a nice, rounded shape.

Knot your string (page 19) and place it into the centre of your pickle, with the knot poking out the top, then pin in place. Secure the string to the top of the pickle with a few stitches.

Starting at the top of the pickle, sew down the final seam, stopping approximately 3 cm (1¼ inch) before the end. Turn your pickle right-side out, using the string to help you.

Stuff your pickle until nice and plump, then use ladder stitch (page 12) to close your final seam.

Using the seams as an entry point for your needle and thread, sew French knots (page 13) all over your pickle to create those signature pickle lumps and bumps, then tie off your thread.

Voila! A Lucky Pickle!

CRACKER STACK

Pile up your favourites with this cheeky little serving suggestion.
The Cracker Stack doubles as a festive party favour,
perfect for the holiday season.

WHAT YOU WILL NEED

- ◯ Tracing paper
- ◯ Pencil
- ◯ Scissors
- ◯ Red felt
- ◯ Pink felt
- ◯ Yellow felt
- ◯ Brown felt
- ◯ Strawboard or a bit of cardboard box
- ◯ Plastic eyes and washers
- ◯ Needle
- ◯ Black thread
- ◯ White thread
- ◯ Red thread
- ◯ A handful of stuffing
- ◯ Pins
- ◯ Brown thread
- ◯ Waxed string
- ◯ PVA glue

Trace and cut your Cracker Stack felt and cardboard pieces from the template (page 132).

Take one cabana face piece and use scissors to help insert the eyes and fasten the washers (page 16). Use black thread to stitch a mouth, then use white thread to stitch some little freckles.

Use red thread and blanket stitch (page 12) to sew the cabana rind onto the cabana face. Sew together the ends of the rind, then add the second pink circle, leaving a small gap for the stuffing.

Stuff the cabana, then close the seam with blanket stitch and tie off your thread.

Gather your two felt cracker pieces and the cardboard insert. Align the two crackers and pin them into place. Use brown thread and blanket stitch to sew around the scalloped edge of the crackers, stopping halfway to insert the cardboard.

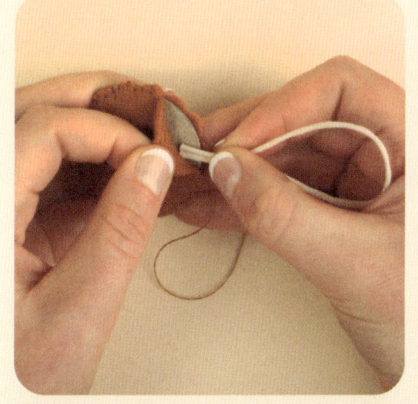

Close up the seam, leaving a small gap to insert the unknotted string.
Fold the string in half and tuck the ends into the gap, then sew through the cracker and string in your last few stitches and tie off your thread.

Use PVA glue to stack your cracker, layering the cheese, then the cabana on top. Press the layers together and allow to dry.
Wow! You have made a fluffy canape worthy of any centrepiece.

BFF CHEESES

One for you, one for a friend.
Cement any friendship with these BFF Cheeses.

WHAT YOU WILL NEED

- ( ) Tracing paper
- ( ) Pencil
- ( ) Scissors
- ( ) Red felt
- ( ) Yellow felt
- ( ) Needle
- ( ) Black thread
- ( ) White thread
- ( ) Yellow thread
- ( ) Red thread
- ( ) 2 x waxed string
- ( ) Pins
- ( ) A handful of stuffing

BONUS!

Swap out
the colours for
BFF Brie cheeses!

Trace and cut your cheese pieces from the template (page 133).

Gather both yellow inner-cheese pieces.

Use black thread to stitch a face onto the right-hand side of each piece, then use white thread to stitch a few little freckles.

Take one inner-cheese piece and fold it in half so the face is turning inwards, then use yellow thread and blanket stitch (page 12) along the fold to create a corner. Fold the second piece so the face is turning outwards, then stitch in the same way.

This will give your cheeses a sharp outward and inward point.

Gather the big cheese rind pieces, then use red thread and blanket stitch to sew the long edge of your big rind strip to one of the rind pieces. Tie off the thread at the end of the seam.

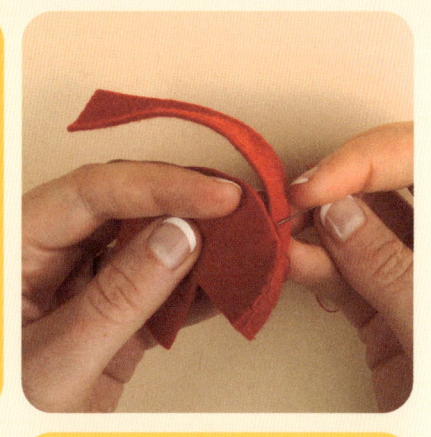

Knot your string (page 19) and pin it, with the knot poking out, to the open edge of the long rind strip.

Use blanket stitch to sew the remaining rind piece in the same fashion as the top, and secure the string with a few stitches as you pass by.

Turn your big cheese rind right-side out and stuff.

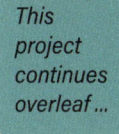 

This project continues overleaf ...

Take the inner cheese piece with the face turning inward, and snuggle it into the opening of the big cheese rind.

To keep everything in place while you stitch, pin through the centre where the inverted corners meet.

Using yellow thread and blanket stitch, sew your cheese face into place. Tie off your thread.

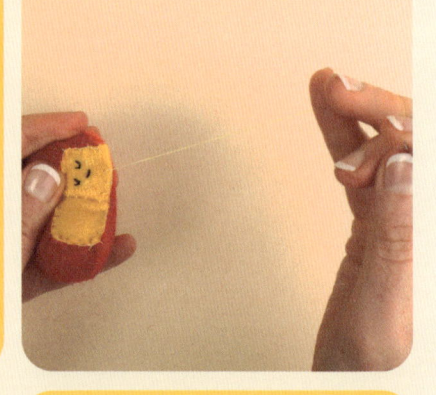

Gather your small cheese felt pieces and the second piece of string; these will make up the missing cheese wedge.

Use red thread and blanket stitch to sew your small cheese rind following the instructions for the large cheese rind (page 35), making sure to secure your string with a few stitches as you close up your second seam. Bonus: a smaller cheese means less stitching this time!

Turn your small cheese rind right-side out, but don't stuff it just yet.

Take the remaining inner-cheese face and pin it between the pointed ends of the rind.

Use yellow thread and blanket stitch to sew your cheese wedge together, stopping on the final corner to stuff, then close up the seam and tie off your thread.

Give one of your cheeses to a kindred spirit: you are now fromage friends forever.

BABY MAYO

Every snack needs a condiment, and so does every handbag!
Switch up the colours and you can have a whole selection
of sauces to apply to any ensemble.

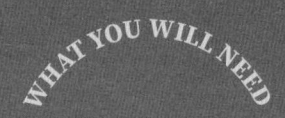

WHAT YOU WILL NEED

- ◯ Tracing paper
- ◯ Pencil
- ◯ Scissors
- ◯ White felt
- ◯ Red felt
- ◯ Needle
- ◯ Black thread
- ◯ Pink thread
- ◯ Pins
- ◯ White thread
- ◯ A handful of stuffing
- ◯ Red thread
- ◯ Waxed string

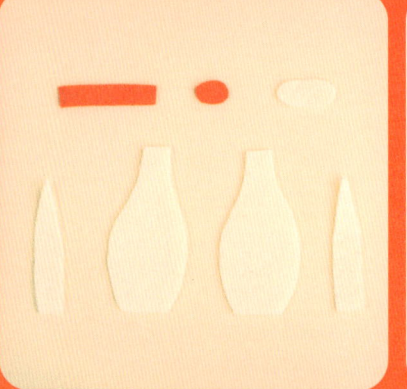

Trace and cut your Baby Mayo pieces from the template (page 133).

Use black thread to sew a face onto one of the bottle-shaped pieces, then use pink thread to stitch some rosy cheeks.

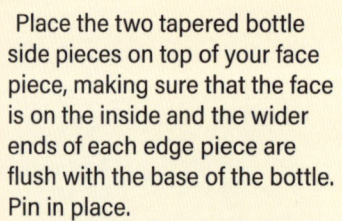

Place the two tapered bottle side pieces on top of your face piece, making sure that the face is on the inside and the wider ends of each edge piece are flush with the base of the bottle. Pin in place.

Using white thread and blanket stitch (page 12), sew the side pieces to the outer edges of the bottle.

Take your second bottle piece and pin one edge to a side piece, making sure that the face is turning inwards and both bottle pieces are aligned. Using blanket stitch, sew up the unpinned side and tie off your thread, then repeat on the other side. Make sure to leave the base and top open for now.

Turn the bottle right-side out and stuff until nice and plump.

Use white thread and blanket stitch to sew the base piece to the bottom of your bottle, then tie off your thread.

A pencil helps turn out and stuff the narrower parts of the bottle.

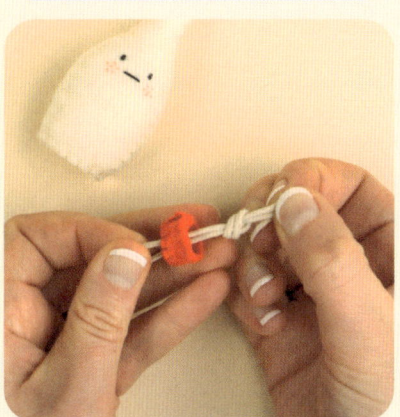

Use red thread and blanket stitch to sew the short edges of the red rectangle together, then stitch on the top of the cap. Turn right-side out.

Knot your string (page 19), then cut a small incision in the top of the cap and thread the looped end of your string through the hole, so the knot sits snuggly inside the cap.

Use your needle and red thread to secure the string into the underside of the cap, then tuck the ends of the string inside the top of the bottle. Use red thread and whip stitch (page 13) to attach the cap to the bottle, then tie off your thread.

Baby Mayo at your service!

Fruit Bowl

Sew up your five a day with this bowl of fruity friends.

Peach Pal

Banana Buddy

Cute Kiwi

Aloof Apple

Sweet Orange

PEACH PAL

Everything's peachy with this tiny, sweet face looking back at you.
Why not make two peach halves and give one to
a peachy pal of your own?

WHAT YOU WILL NEED

- ◯ Tracing paper
- ◯ Pencil
- ◯ Scissors
- ◯ Brown felt
- ◯ Light pink or peach felt
- ◯ Light orange felt
- ◯ Green felt
- ◯ Needle
- ◯ Black thread
- ◯ Pink thread
- ◯ Brown thread
- ◯ Orange thread
- ◯ A handful of stuffing
- ◯ Waxed string
- ◯ Pins

Trace and cut your peach pieces from the template (page 134).

Use black thread to stitch a friendly face onto your little brown peach stone, then use pink thread to stitch some tiny, rosy cheeks.

Use brown thread and whip stitch (page 13) to attach the face to the peach centre. When you are just shy of the end, add a little stuffing to puff out your stone — you can use a pencil to help poke the stuffing in there!

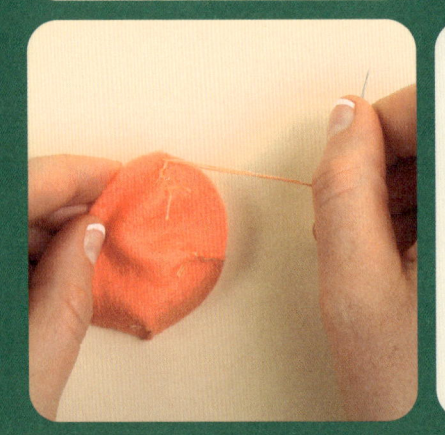

Use pink thread and blanket stitch to sew up the three darts on the outer peach.

Turn it out so the stitches are on the inside — this will give you a nice, rounded peach.

The opening on your outer peach should now just about match the size of your peach face, but if not, you can always stretch the felt a little to fit!

Place the peach pieces together, with the face and the rounded point of the outer peach facing away from one another.

Start from the top and use orange thread and blanket stitch to sew up the seam. When you are about three-quarters of the way around, pause your stitching and stuff your peach until plump.

Tie a looped knot with your waxed string (page 19) and pin it, with the knot sitting just inside the top of the peach.

Sew up the seam, making sure to secure the string with the last couple of stitches.

Before tying off your thread, use it to attach the tiny little leaf atop the peach, in front of the string.

Tie off your thread and give yourself a pat on the back — you made a peach!

ALOOF APPLE

This half of an apple is a whole lot of cute.
A friendly face to offer to a favourite teacher
or accompany you to the dentist.

WHAT YOU WILL NEED

- ○ Tracing paper
- ○ Pencil
- ○ Scissors
- ○ White felt
- ○ Red felt
- ○ Brown felt
- ○ Green felt
- ○ Needle
- ○ Black thread
- ○ Pink thread
- ○ Red thread
- ○ White thread
- ○ A handful of stuffing
- ○ Waxed string
- ○ Pins
- ○ Brown thread

Trace and cut your apple pieces from the template (page 134).

Use black thread to apply a face to the white part of your apple, then use pink thread to stitch some rosy cheeks.

Use red thread and blanket stitch to sew up the three the darts on the the red felt piece. Once all three seams are closed, turn it out so the stitches are on the inside — this will give you a nice, rounded apple.

The opening of your apple skin should just about match the size of your apple face.

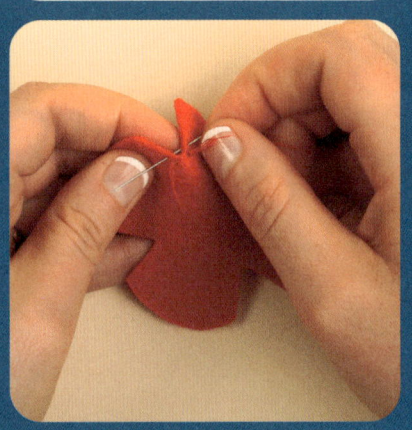

Place your apple face and apple skin pieces on top of one another, with both the face and the rounded point of the skin facing outwards.

Starting from the top, use white thread and blanket stitch to sew your apple face and apple skin together. When you are three-quarters of the way around, pause your stitching and stuff your apple.

Knot your string (page 19) and pin it, with the knot sitting just inside the top of your apple.

Close up the seam, making sure to secure the string with the last couple of stitches. Tie off your thread.

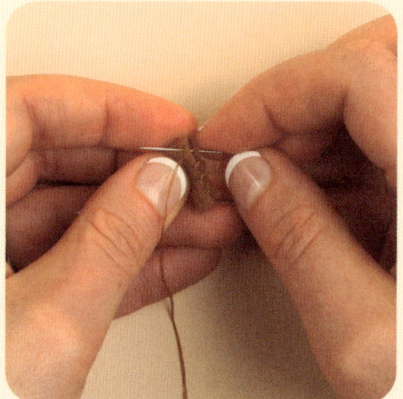

Roll the small brown felt piece into a stalk-ish shape and use brown thread and whip stitch (page 13) to sew up the side. Attach the stalk behind the string of your apple with a couple of stitches and tie off.

Finally, add the green leaf to the base of the stalk with a couple of small stitches and tie off the thread.

Apple complete!

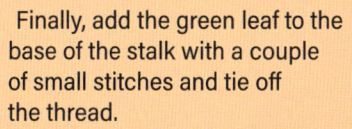

CUTE KIWI

Fuzzy, green and as good for your health as the real thing (probably!).
This kiwi is sure to bring a smile to a sweet friend.

WHAT YOU WILL NEED

- ◯ Tracing paper
- ◯ Pencil
- ◯ Scissors
- ◯ White felt
- ◯ Green felt
- ◯ Brown felt
- ◯ Needle
- ◯ Black thread
- ◯ Pink thread
- ◯ Brown thread
- ◯ A handful of stuffing
- ◯ Waxed string
- ◯ Pins

Trace and cut your kiwi pieces from the template (page 135).

Use black thread to apply a face to the small white circle piece of your kiwi, then use pink thread to stitch some rosy cheeks.

Use black thread and whip stitch (page 13) to sew the face of the kiwi to the green felt.

Use a long stitch on the first go-round, then, for a decorative touch, insert smaller stitches on the second go-round.

Use brown thread and blanket stitch (page 12) to sew up the darts on the kiwi skin, then turn it out so the stitches are on the inside — this will create a nice, rounded shape.

Place your green face on top of the opening of the kiwi skin — they should be the same size, or just about.

If it looks like one piece is much bigger than the other, you can always stretch your felt a little to fit!

Starting at the top of your kiwi, use brown thread and blanket stitch to sew the face and kiwi skin together. When you are three-quarters of the way around, pop in the stuffing, a little at a time, until it's nice and plump.

Knot your string (page 19) and pin it, with the knot sitting just inside the top of your kiwi. Now close up the seam, making sure to secure the string with the last couple of stitches.

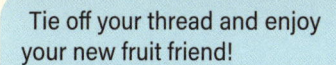

Tie off your thread and enjoy your new fruit friend!

BANANA BUDDY

A bewildered banana that won't get
forgotten at the bottom of your backpack.
Bruised to your liking (or make it green if you're that way inclined!).

WHAT YOU WILL NEED

- ◯ Tracing paper
- ◯ Pencil
- ◯ Scissors
- ◯ Yellow felt
- ◯ Needle
- ◯ Yellow thread
- ◯ Plastic eyes and washers
- ◯ Black thread
- ◯ Pink thread
- ◯ A handful of stuffing
- ◯ Waxed string
- ◯ Pins
- ◯ Brown embroidery thread

Trace and cut your banana pieces from the template (page 135).

Place the two banana side pieces on top of each other. Starting at the top of the flatter side of the banana pieces, use yellow thread and blanket stitch (page 12) to sew three stitches — this will be your stalk.

Add the petal-shaped piece into the centre of your banana, below the stalk, then use blanket stitch to sew up both seams.

Turn your banana right-side over and poke the eyes into the seams (no snipping required) and secure with washers at the back. Use black thread to stitch a mouth, then pink thread to stitch some rosy cheeks.

Curl the sides of your banana together so the face is on the inside, then use yellow thread and blanket stitch to sew up the final seam from the bottom tip. Stop a little over halfway up and turn the banana right-side out.

Stuff your banana until nice and plump, using a pencil to get into the small, pointy end.

Fold your waxed string in half and pin it, unknotted, into the inside tip of your banana.

Use yellow thread and ladder stitch (page 12) to close the seam shut, making sure to secure the string with the last couple of stitches before tying off your thread.

Using brown embroidery thread, wind it around the stalk, then sew tiny stitches over the butt of your banana. Use freestyle stitch (page 13) to add little brown bits all over — you can go for lightly bruised, heavily bruised, or lost at the bottom of the bag, now unrecognisable and not-even-fit-for-banana-bread bruised — whatever your preference!

SWEET ORANGE

Round, cute and comforting!
This sizeable and juicy citrus friend will ensure
you never lose your keys again!

WHAT YOU WILL NEED

- ◯ Tracing paper
- ◯ Pencil
- ◯ Scissors
- ◯ Orange felt
- ◯ Green felt
- ◯ Needle
- ◯ Plastic eyes and washers
- ◯ Black thread
- ◯ Pink thread
- ◯ Orange thread
- ◯ A handful of stuffing
- ◯ Waxed string
- ◯ Pins

Trace and cut your orange pieces from the template (page 135).

Take one orange segment and insert the plastic eyes and washers (page 16) about a third of the way down. Use black thread to stitch a mouth, then use pink thread to stitch some rosy cheeks.

Place one of the orange segments on top of the face piece, with the face on the inside, then use orange thread and blanket stitch (page 12) to sew down one side.

Once you arrive at the bottom tip of the orange with your first seam, join the third segment in on the other side, easing around the curves as you stitch. When you reach the top, add the final segment and stitch to halfway along the seam.

Use the gap you have just left in the seam to turn your orange right-side out.

Stuff your orange until nice and plump.

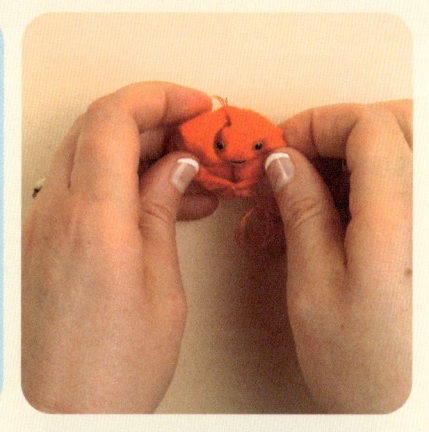

Knot your string (page 19), then insert the knot into the top of the orange where the tips of the segments join and pin in place.

Use orange thread and ladder stitch (page 12) to sew the seam shut, making sure to secure the string with the last couple of stitches.

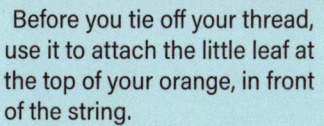

Before you tie off your thread, use it to attach the little leaf at the top of your orange, in front of the string.

Using the seams as an entry point, sew orange French knots (page 13) all over your orange to give a nice bumpy look to your new citrus pal.

Eggs Three Ways

Breakfast is served with an egg for all occasions.

Soft Boiled

Sunny Side Up

On Toast

SOFT BOILED

Soft, friendly and a perfect breakfast snack.
For that good egg in your life.

WHAT YOU WILL NEED

- ( ) Tracing paper
- ( ) Pencil
- ( ) Scissors
- ( ) Yellow felt
- ( ) Light brown felt
- ( ) White felt
- ( ) Needle
- ( ) Black thread
- ( ) Pink thread
- ( ) Yellow thread
- ( ) Light brown thread
- ( ) Waxed string
- ( ) Pins
- ( ) White thread
- ( ) A handful of stuffing

BONUS!

Switch up the colours and you have yourself an Agreeable Avocado!

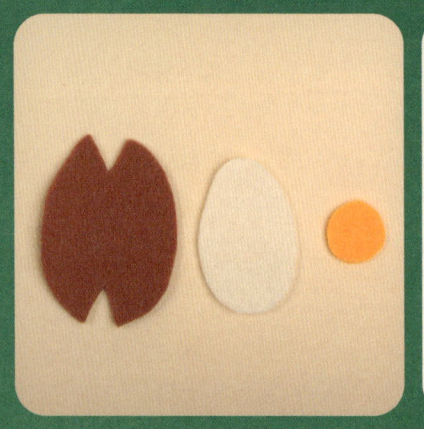

Trace and cut your boiled egg pieces from the template (page 136).

Use black thread to add a face to your yolk, then pink thread to stitch some rosy cheeks.

Place the yolk, face-side up, on the lower, wider part of your egg white, then use yellow thread and whip stitch (page 13) to sew them together.

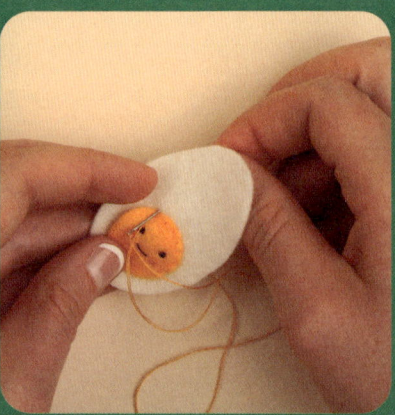

Use light brown thread and blanket stitch to sew up the two darts on your eggshell. Turn out the eggshell so the stitches are on the inside — this should give it a nice, rounded shape.

Tie a looped knot with your waxed string (page 19) and sandwich it between the shell and the white, securing with pins at the top and bottom. It may look like the shell is too big for the white, but don't worry, the pins will keep you on track!

Use white thread and blanket stitch to sew your egg together, making sure to secure the string in your stitches at the start.

When you are three-quarters of the way along, stop stitching and start stuffing, then close up the seam and tie off your thread.

Behold, your perfectly soft-boiled egg!

SUNNY SIDE UP

Keep on the sunny side with this friendly, free-form egg.
Store one in your handbag to whip out as an emergency
cheer-up present in a crisis!

WHAT YOU WILL NEED

- ◯ Tracing paper
- ◯ Pencil
- ◯ Scissors
- ◯ Yellow felt
- ◯ White felt
- ◯ Needle
- ◯ Black thread
- ◯ Pink thread
- ◯ Yellow thread
- ◯ A pinch of stuffing
- ◯ Waxed string
- ◯ Pins
- ◯ White thread

Trace and cut your fried egg pieces from the template (page 136).

Use black thread to stitch a happy face onto your yolk, then use pink thread to stitch some rosy cheeks.

Position your yolk on one of the egg white pieces, then use yellow thread and blanket stitch (page 12) to sew together. Pause your stitching when you are just shy of the end to add a little stuffing and plump up your yolk — a pencil helps! Close up the seam and tie off your thread.

Knot your string (page 19) and then make an egg sandwich by layering your blank egg white, your looped string (with the knot poking out the top), and your just-stitched yolk, face-side down, on top of each other. Align the egg whites and pin that sandwich together, stat!

Starting to one side of the string, use white thread and blanket stitch to sew around your inverted egg, making sure to stitch through the string a few times so it's nicely secured. Pause your stitches three-quarters of the way around.

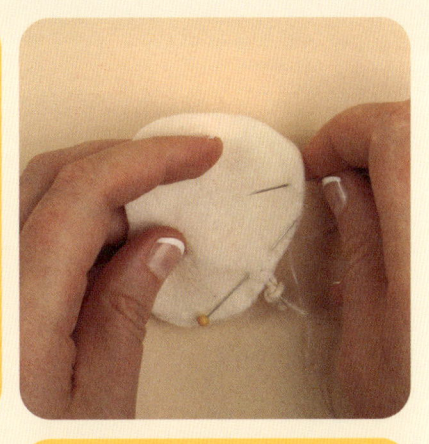

Turn your egg right-side out.

Use ladder stitch (page 12) to sew the seam shut — there's no need to stuff, fried eggs are pretty flat!

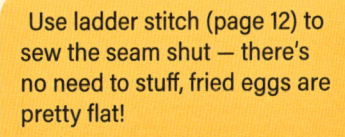

ON TOAST

Egg, meet toast: the perfect pairing.
This basic brilliant breakfast favourite is ready for your
customisation: think pepper sprinkles and a parsley garnish!

WHAT YOU WILL NEED

- ◯ Tracing paper
- ◯ Pencil
- ◯ Scissors
- ◯ White felt
- ◯ Yellow felt
- ◯ Needle
- ◯ Black thread
- ◯ Pink thread
- ◯ Yellow thread
- ◯ A handful of stuffing
- ◯ Waxed string
- ◯ Pins
- ◯ White thread
- ◯ Brown felt
- ◯ Beige felt
- ◯ Light brown thread
- ◯ PVA glue

Follow the Sunny Side Up instructions (pages 74–75) to make your egg, then trace and cut your toast pieces from the template (page 137).

Use light brown thread and blanket stitch (page 12) to sew the crust to one of the bread shapes — the crust should align at a perpendicular angle to the bread shape as shown.

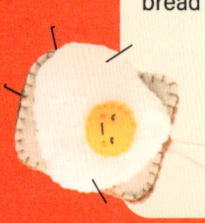

Work in your second bread shape on the other side of the crust, and stitch together in the same fashion, stopping near the end to lightly stuff your now-thick slice of toast.

Continue with blanket stitch to close up your slice of toast, then use whip stitch (page 13) to sew the short edges of the crust together.

Take your egg and apply a good squiggle of PVA glue on the base of your egg. Flip it over and, making sure your toast and egg are oriented the same way, glue your egg onto the toast.

Press down and give your egg and toast some alone time to get fully stuck to each other.
Breakfast is served!

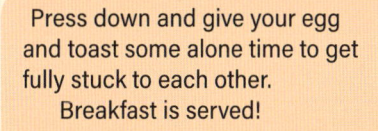

Meal
Deal

Grab a combo of convenience-store staples and head to the park for a sunny lunchtime break.

Salad Sando

Packet O' Crisps

Bottle O' Juice

SALAD SANDO

A garden-variety sandwich
to jazz up a garden-variety workday.
A perfect gift for your work lunch buddy.

WHAT YOU WILL NEED

- ◯ Tracing paper
- ◯ Pencil
- ◯ Scissors
- ◯ White felt
- ◯ Brown felt
- ◯ Green felt
- ◯ Yellow felt
- ◯ Plastic eyes and washers
- ◯ Needle
- ◯ White thread
- ◯ Black thread
- ◯ A handful of stuffing
- ◯ Waxed string
- ◯ Pins

Trace and cut your sandwich pieces from the template (page 138).

Take the inner crusts and use scissors to snip a small hole about a quarter of the way down each crust, where you'd like the eyes to sit. Insert the eyes and fasten with the washers.

Like this!

Use white thread and blanket stitch (page 12) to sew one long edge of an inner crust to the long edge of a bread triangle. Sew a second triangle in the same way, making sure the tips of the triangles match up.

Repeat the steps above to create your second sandwich half, making sure both eyes are roughly aligned.

Use black thread to make a few tiny stitches under each eye, creating some pepper freckles.

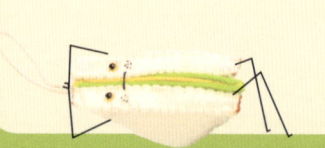

Use white thread and blanket stitch to sew the brown crusts to your bread triangles. Pause your stitching when you near the end and lightly stuff your triangles. Sew the seams shut and tie off your thread. (This is a lot of stitching, so maybe have a cup of tea and walk around the block between slices.)

Make a lettuce—cheese—lettuce stack, making sure the flat sides are all aligned.

Fold your waxed string in half and pin the ends to each side of the corner tip of your filling.

Stitch through the filling and string a few times to secure them. Don't worry, you won't see the stitches — they are purely practical!

Sandwich your bread and filling in a stack and, using the seam as an entry point, make big secure stitches through the entire sandwich, to keep it all together. Tie off. Do this at each pointed end (so, three times).

Use black thread to stitch a mouth from one side of the bread to the other, then tie off your thread.

Like this. And now you're ready for lunch!

PACKET O' CRISPS

A comforting snack to see you through a long afternoon.
Whether you prefer cheese and onion, barbecue or just plain salted,
you can add your own flavour to this salty snack.

WHAT YOU WILL NEED

- ◯ Tracing paper
- ◯ Pencil
- ◯ Scissors
- ◯ Light brown felt
- ◯ Green felt
- ◯ Blue felt
- ◯ Needle
- ◯ Black thread
- ◯ Light brown thread
- ◯ White thread
- ◯ Red thread
- ◯ Pins
- ◯ A handful of stuffing
- ◯ Waxed string

Trace and cut your crisp packet pieces from the template (page 139).

Use black thread to sew a face onto the tiny potato shape, then use brown thread to add a few freckles.

Use brown thread to whip stitch (page 13) the potato to the centre of the green circle, then use white thread to whip stitch the circle to the blue crisp packet.

Once your pieces are sewn together, you can get decorative with your stitches — I've sewn big red stitches between each small white stitch.

Place your freshly stitched piece face-down on the other blue crisp packet piece, aligning the edges, then use blue thread and blanket stitch (page 12) to sew up the sides. Leave the ends open.

Turn your crisp packet right-side out, then align one of the green strips with the bottom of the crisp packet and pin in place.

Use red thread and blanket stitch to sew all three layers together, closing up the bottom seam in the process. Fold the bottom green strip downwards.

Stuff your crisp packet!

Fold the string in half and tuck the two loose ends into the top of your crisp packet. Align the second green strip with the top of the packet and pin all three layers of felt, plus the string, in place. Use red thread and blanket stitch to sew the packet closed, adding a few extra stitches over the string for good measure. Fold the top green strip upwards.

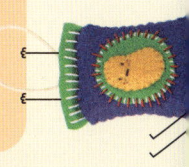

Use white thread to add some decorative stitches to the edges as shown.

A sassy felt snack is now at your disposal!

BOTTLE O'JUICE

A fruity tipple to dangle from your purse.

Don't like orange? No worries! Use your creative
flair to switch up the flavours and colours.

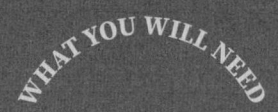

WHAT YOU WILL NEED

- ◯ Tracing paper
- ◯ Pencil
- ◯ Scissors
- ◯ Bright orange felt
- ◯ Light blue felt
- ◯ Dark orange felt
- ◯ Green felt
- ◯ Needle
- ◯ Black thread
- ◯ Pink thread
- ◯ Orange thread
- ◯ Pins
- ◯ A handful of stuffing
- ◯ Green thread
- ◯ Waxed string

Trace and cut your juice pieces from the template (page 139).

Use black thread to stitch a face to the smallest orange circle, then use pink thread to stitch some rosy freckles.

Place the face in the centre of the blue rectangle and use orange thread and whip stitch (page 13) to sew the face onto the label, adding the green leaf before the final few stitches.

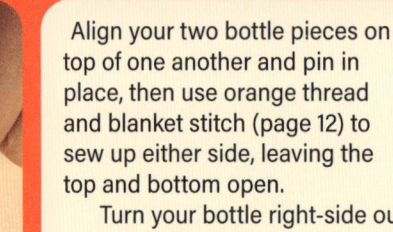

Align your two bottle pieces on top of one another and pin in place, then use orange thread and blanket stitch (page 12) to sew up either side, leaving the top and bottom open.

Turn your bottle right-side out and stuff, using a pencil to reach into the narrower parts.

Use blanket stitch to sew the round base to the bottom of your bottle, then tie off your thread.

Use orange thread and whip stitch to sew the short edges of the blue label to your bottle, making sure the label is centred between the side seams of the bottle — the edges should just overshoot each seam.

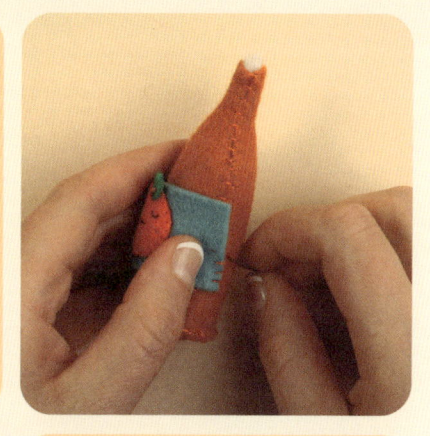

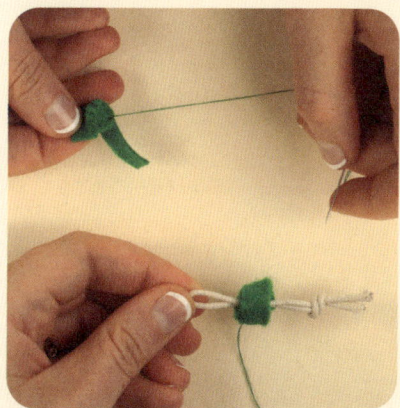

Take the green rectangle and use green thread and blanket stitch to sew the bottle cap by joining the short edges, then sew the green circle on top.

Tie a looped knot with your string (page 19), then make a small incision in the top of the cap and pass the looped end of the string through — give it a gentle tug so the knot sits snuggly inside the cap.

Use green thread to sew a few stitches across the string in the underside of the cap, to secure the string in place. Tuck the string ends into the top of the bottle, then use green thread and whip stitch to sew the cap to the bottle. Tie off your thread.

Your drink is ready — bottoms up!

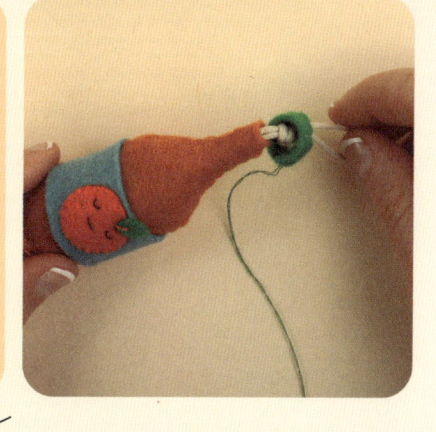

A Day
at the
Fair

No trip to the fairground is complete without a visit to the hot food van.

Bucket O' Chips

HOT
CHIPS

HOT
DONUTS

Cotton Candy

Hot
Donut

COTTON CANDY

Fluffy, pink and the perfect gift for a sweetheart.
This project uses a needle felting technique to
achieve the puffiest snack possible!

WHAT YOU WILL NEED

- ◯ Tracing paper
- ◯ Pencil
- ◯ Scissors
- ◯ Pink felt
- ◯ Pink wool roving
- ◯ Felting needle
- ◯ Short wooden skewer, around 10 cm (4 inches) long
- ◯ Waxed string
- ◯ Pins
- ◯ Needle
- ◯ Pink thread
- ◯ A handful of stuffing
- ◯ PVA glue
- ◯ Plastic eyes
- ◯ Black thread

IMPORTANT FUZZY NOTE!

Wool roving and a felting needle are the key to creating a puffy, cloud-like cotton candy.

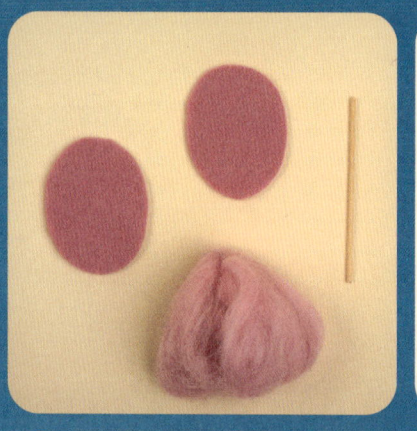

Trace and cut your two cotton candy pieces from the template (page 140), and gather your pink wool roving, felting needle and wooden skewer.

Knot your string (page 19), then place it between your cotton candy pieces, with the knot poking out the top. Pin in place.

Using pink thread and blanket stitch (page 12), start at the top to secure your string with a few stitches, then sew around the outside, stopping when you are three-quarters of the way along.

Turn the felt right-side out, then stuff until nice and plump.

Close up the seam with ladder stitch (page 12), then tie off your thread.

Pop some glue onto one end of your skewer and wiggle it into the seam at the base of your cotton candy. Wait a few moments while it sticks into place.

Take you pink wool roving and gently form it into an even-ish shape that is big enough to cover your cotton candy base. Wrap the roving around the base and repeatedly poke your felting needle through both the roving and base, until you've covered the entire surface area. This step adheres the fluff to your felt base and the more you poke, the more solid the shape will become.

Be careful of your fingers and make sure you do this step at a desk and not on your lap — it's easy to get carried away with the sharp needle!

Use scissors to snip two small incisions, then pop your cotton candy down for a moment while you dab a small amount of glue to the stalk of each eye. Insert each eye, making sure to push them in firmly, then leave for a few minutes to dry.

Use black thread to stitch a mouth, then pink thread to sew some sugary cheeks.
One sweet new fluffy friend has appeared!

HOT DONUT

Who can resist a fluffy cinnamon donut?
Make it for a friend and customise the
bag in their honour!

WHAT YOU WILL NEED

- ◯ Tracing paper
- ◯ Pencil
- ◯ Scissors
- ◯ Brown felt
- ◯ White felt
- ◯ Plastic eyes and washers
- ◯ Needle
- ◯ Black thread
- ◯ White thread
- ◯ Waxed string
- ◯ Pins
- ◯ Brown thread
- ◯ A handful of stuffing
- ◯ Blue thread
- ◯ Red thread

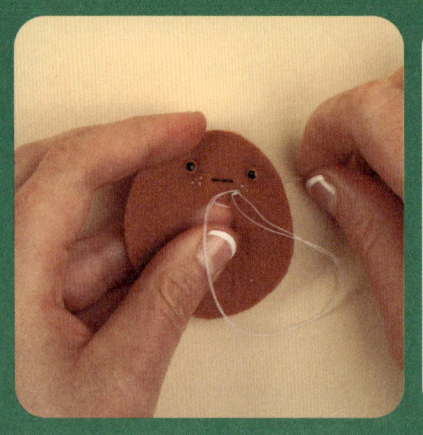

Trace and cut your hot donut pieces from the template (page 140).

Use scissors to help insert the plastic eyes, then fasten with the washers (page 16), then use black thread to stitch a mouth, and white thread to sew some sugar freckles.

Knot your string (page 19), then sandwich your donut pieces together, with the face on the inside, and insert the string into the middle, with the knot poking out the top. Pin into place.

Use brown thread and blanket stitch (page 12) to sew around the outside edge, incorporating the string at the top with a few extra stitches. Tie off your thread.

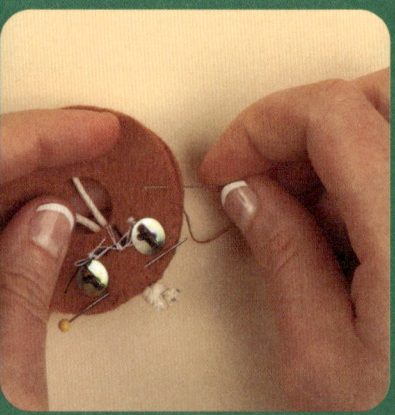

Turn your donut right-side out, then take a deep breath and prepare for some fiddly stitching.

Use brown thread and blanket stitch to sew the inside seam of the donut, carefully adding some stuffing with a pencil as you go. Be patient, go slowly, you can do it!

Now after that bit of tricky stitching, a reward! Use blue and red thread (or whatever colours please you) to freestyle stitch (page 13) one of the donut bag pieces.

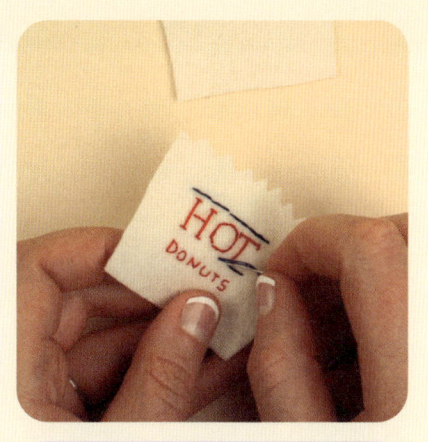

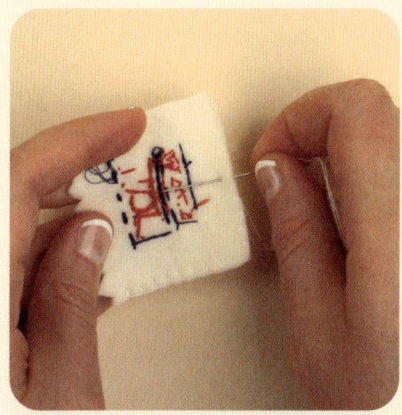

Lay the two bag pieces on top of one another, with the stitched side turned inwards, and use white thread and blanket stitch to sew along the sides and bottom of the bag — make sure to keep the top zigzag edge open.

Tie off your thread, then turn your bag right-side out.

Snuggle your donut into the bag — I find it usually fits well enough and doesn't need stitches to keep it in place, but you can add a few security stitches if you're worried, or if the bag has turned out a little loose.

One Hot Donut is packed and ready to go!

BUCKET O' CHIPS

A moreish bundle of fried friends.
Some mini hot chippies to swing from
your bag; sauce optional.

WHAT YOU WILL NEED

- ◯ Tracing paper
- ◯ Pencil
- ◯ Scissors
- ◯ White felt
- ◯ Red felt
- ◯ Yellow felt
- ◯ Needle
- ◯ Red thread
- ◯ Black thread
- ◯ White thread
- ◯ Pins
- ◯ Yellow thread
- ◯ A handful of stuffing
- ◯ PVA glue

Trace and cut your Bucket O' Chips pieces from the template (page 141).

Use red thread and whip stitch (page 13) to sew the red banner to the middle of the white rectangle. Then, use different colour threads to freestyle stitch (page 13) your chip bucket design — I have used black, red and white.

I believe in you! The wonkier the better, in my humble opinion.

With the label facing you, fold the top edge of the rectangle over to create a 3 mm (1/8 inch) overhang. Pin in place.

Working from the front of your label, use white thread and whip stitch to sew this fold down as shown — this will create the lip of your bucket.

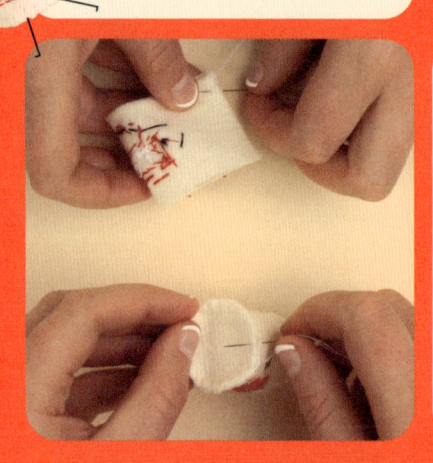

Fold the long edge of your rectangle in half, with the label facing inwards, then use white thread and blanket stitch (page 12) to sew the short edges together, creating a cylinder. Turn the cylinder right-side out, and use blanket stitch to sew the white circle to the base, making sure your label is facing the right way up. Your bucket is ready for some chips!

And now for the chippies! Take five of your yellow chip shapes and use black thread to stitch tiny faces to the top of each piece. Pair each freshly stitched chip face with a blank chip shape. Lay the piece with the face on top of the blank shape and use yellow thread and blanket stitch to sew the two pieces together, stopping about two-thirds of the way to add a little stuffing with a pencil.

You don't need to stitch the bottom of the chips as they will be glued in to the bucket and hidden away.

Fold your string in half and use yellow thread to stitch the unknotted strings ends together at the base.

Bundle all your chippies together, with the faces looking in the same direction and your string at the back of the bunch, then use yellow thread to pass the needle through and around and all about, so your chips and string are in a nice secure clump.

Apply PVA glue to the bottom of your chips and pop them into the bucket. Give your chippies some time to stick into place.

Your Bucket O' Chips is ready for a day at the fair!

Time for Dinner

Craft your perfect bowl of comfort with this trio of dinnertime delights.

Plush Mush

Octo-Sausage

Ebi Fry

PLUSH MUSH

There's always room for a mushroom in your life!
This cute-as-a-button charm is the perfect gift for the
fun-guy in your life.

WHAT YOU WILL NEED

- ◯ Tracing paper
- ◯ Pencil
- ◯ Scissors
- ◯ White felt
- ◯ Beige felt
- ◯ Brown felt
- ◯ Needle
- ◯ Black thread
- ◯ Pink thread
- ◯ Dark brown thread
- ◯ Light brown thread
- ◯ Waxed string
- ◯ A handful of stuffing
- ◯ White thread
- ◯ Pins

Be careful not to pull your gill stitches too tight as it will bunch the felt.

Trace and cut your Plush Mush pieces from the template (page 142).

Use black thread to sew a face onto one side of the stalk, then use pink thread to stitch some rosy cheeks.

Take your beige circle and use dark brown thread to sew long stitches from the centre to the edge, forming the gills.

Use light brown thread and running stitch (page 12) to sew around the edge of your brown mushroom cap.

Gently pull the thread every few stitches to gather the felt until it roughly matches the size of your gill piece. Tie off your thread.

Make a small incision in the centre of your mushroom cap, then knot your string (page 19) and pass the looped end through the hole, with the knot sitting on the underside of the mushroom. Secure the string in place with a couple of small stitches.

Align your gill and cap pieces and use light brown thread and blanket stitch (page 12) to sew them together. This bit can be tricky with all the long loopy gill stitches to navigate past, but persevere! When you're near the end, pause your stitching to stuff your mushroom cap, then close up the seam and tie off your thread.

Return to your stalk and fold it in half, with the face on the inside. Beginning at the base of the stalk, use white thread and blanket stitch to sew along the edge, leaving a gap at the top. Turn your stalk right-side out and stuff until nice and plump, using a pencil to push your stuffing all the way down.

Use white thread and ladder stitch (page 12) to sew up the small, open seam at the top of the folded side of your mushroom stalk. Then, keeping that thread in play, position your stalk in the centre of the underside of your mushroom cap (a pin will help to keep it in place) and use ladder stitch to sew them together.
Fungi finished!

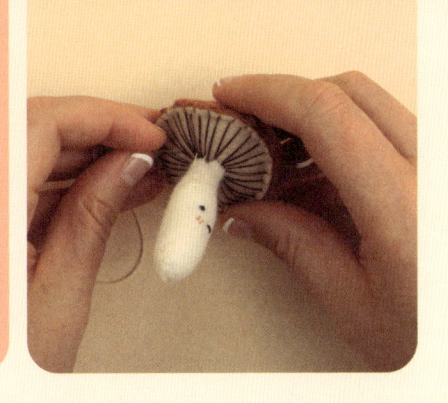

OCTO-SAUSAGE

A sausage cut in such a way so as to resemble an octopus.
To whoever invented this genius idea, hats off to you!

WHAT YOU WILL NEED

- ◯ Tracing paper
- ◯ Pencil
- ◯ Scissors
- ◯ Red felt
- ◯ Pink felt
- ◯ Plastic eyes and washers
- ◯ Needle
- ◯ Black thread
- ◯ Pink thread
- ◯ Red thread
- ◯ Waxed string
- ◯ A handful of stuffing
- ◯ Pins

Trace and cut your Octo-Sausage pieces from the template (page 143).

Take one red felt octo-petal and use scissors to insert the plastic eyes and fasten with the washers (page 16) about a third of the way down. Then, use black thread to stitch a mouth and pink thread to sew some salty freckles.

Lay another octo-petal on top of your face petal, with the face on the inside.

Starting a quarter of the way from the bottom, use red thread and blanket stitch (page 12) to sew up one side to the top, easing around the curved felt as you go.

Once you reach the top, knot your string (page 19), then sandwich it between your petals, with the knot poking out the top, and secure the string with a few small stitches.

Add in your final octo-petal and, starting at the top, use blanket stitch to sew the remaining two seams — we are leaving the bottom of the petals open, for now.

Tie off your thread, then turn your octo-friend right-side out and stuff until nice and plump.

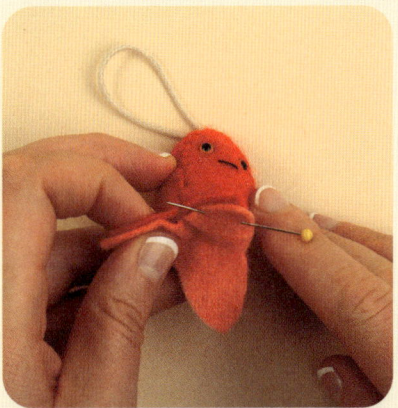

Take your pink felt piece and line it up with the open petals at the bottom of your Octo-Sausage. Align each tentacle point and pin in place.

You may need to stretch and ease the felt to line up the tentacles.

Use red thread and blanket stitch to sew the pink and red felt together, adding a little extra stuffing into each tentacle point as you go.

An Octo-Sausage is born!

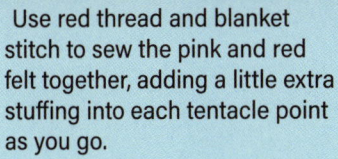

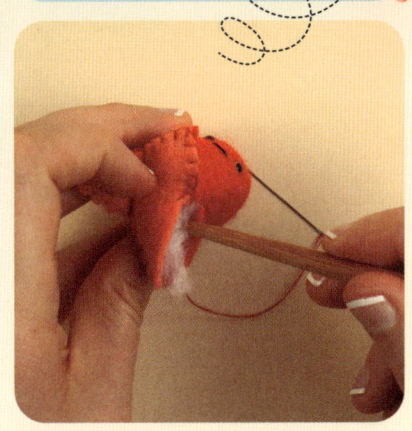

EBI FRY

This is seafood at its fried, felty best!
Use a fluffy fabric to give this little crispy friend
a perfectly crumbed complexion.

WHAT YOU WILL NEED

- ◯ Tracing paper
- ◯ Pencil
- ◯ Scissors
- ◯ Beige or light yellow fuzzy felt or a woolly textured fabric
- ◯ Orange felt
- ◯ Plastic eyes and washers
- ◯ Needle
- ◯ Black thread
- ◯ Pink thread
- ◯ Cream thread
- ◯ Waxed string
- ◯ A handful of stuffing
- ◯ Orange thread
- ◯ Pins

Trace and cut your prawn pieces from the template (page 143).

Take one of the textured prawn pieces and use scissors to help insert the eyes and fasten with the washers (page 16), towards the top, wider end. Use black thread to sew a mouth, and pink thread and a few straight stitches to form some rosy cheeks.

Lay a second textured piece on top of your face piece, with the face on the inside — if your fabric has a right and wrong side, make sure the right side (i.e., fluffy side) is turning inwards at this stage.

Leaving the base open, start at the bottom of the prawn and use cream thread and blanket stitch (page 12) to sew to the top, easing around the curved felt.

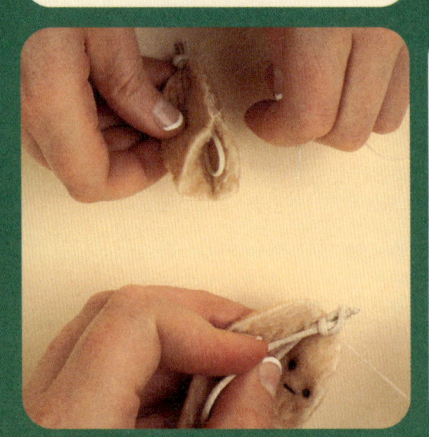

Knot your string (page 19) and place it between the prawn pieces, with the knot poking out the top, then secure your string with a few tiny stitches.

Add the third prawn piece and use blanket stitch to sew down the second seam. Stitch the final seam in the same way, making sure to keep the bottom of the prawn open.

Turn your prawn right-side out and stuff until nice and plump.

Take your prawn tail pieces and use orange thread and blanket stitch to sew them together, leaving the top open. It's a tiny piece, so you'll want to stuff a little at a time, employing that handy pencil to assist you!

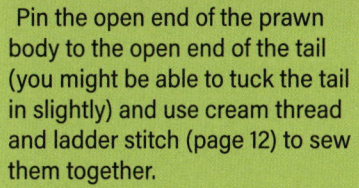

Pin the open end of the prawn body to the open end of the tail (you might be able to tuck the tail in slightly) and use cream thread and ladder stitch (page 12) to sew them together.

And there you have it, a fried ebi to dangle from your satchel!

TEMPLATES

NIBBLE PLATTER

LUCKY PICKLE

Use tracing paper, a pencil and some scissors to draw and cut your required pattern pieces. Label them with your pencil, so you can easily remember what's what. Store your tracing paper pattern pieces in an obliging envelope so you can use them again and again!

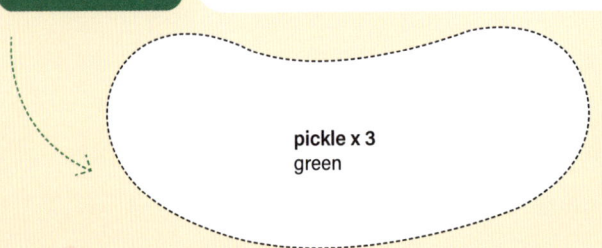

pickle x 3
green

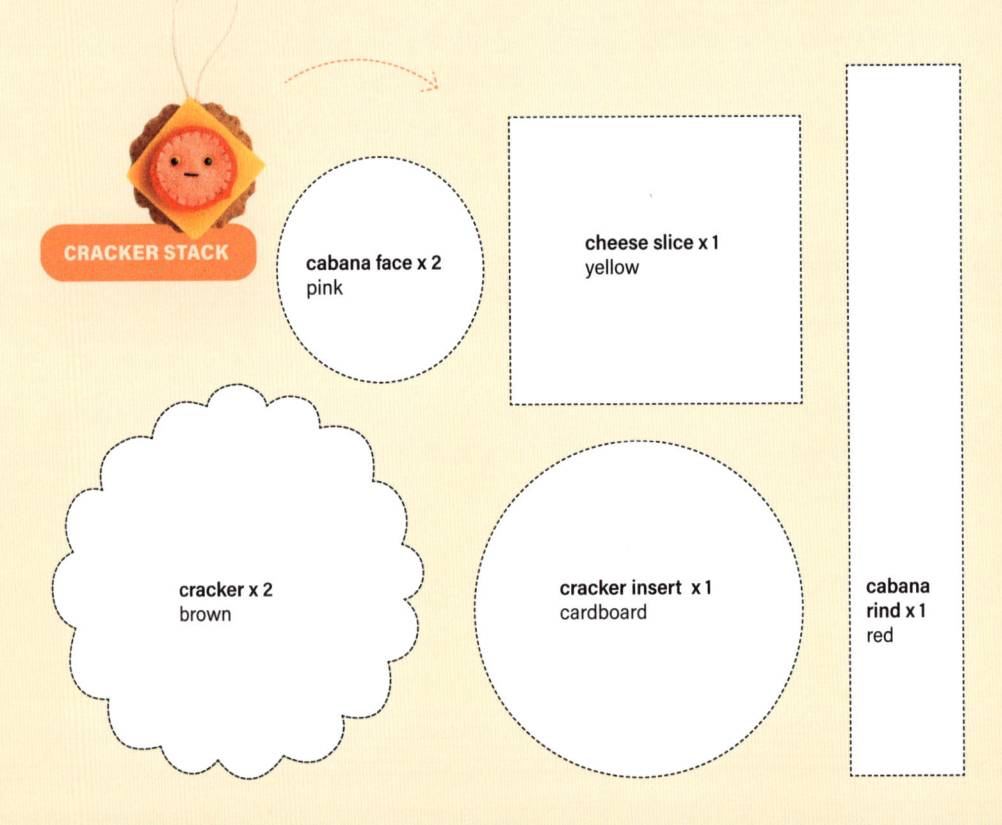

CRACKER STACK

cabana face x 2
pink

cheese slice x 1
yellow

cracker x 2
brown

cracker insert x 1
cardboard

cabana rind x 1
red

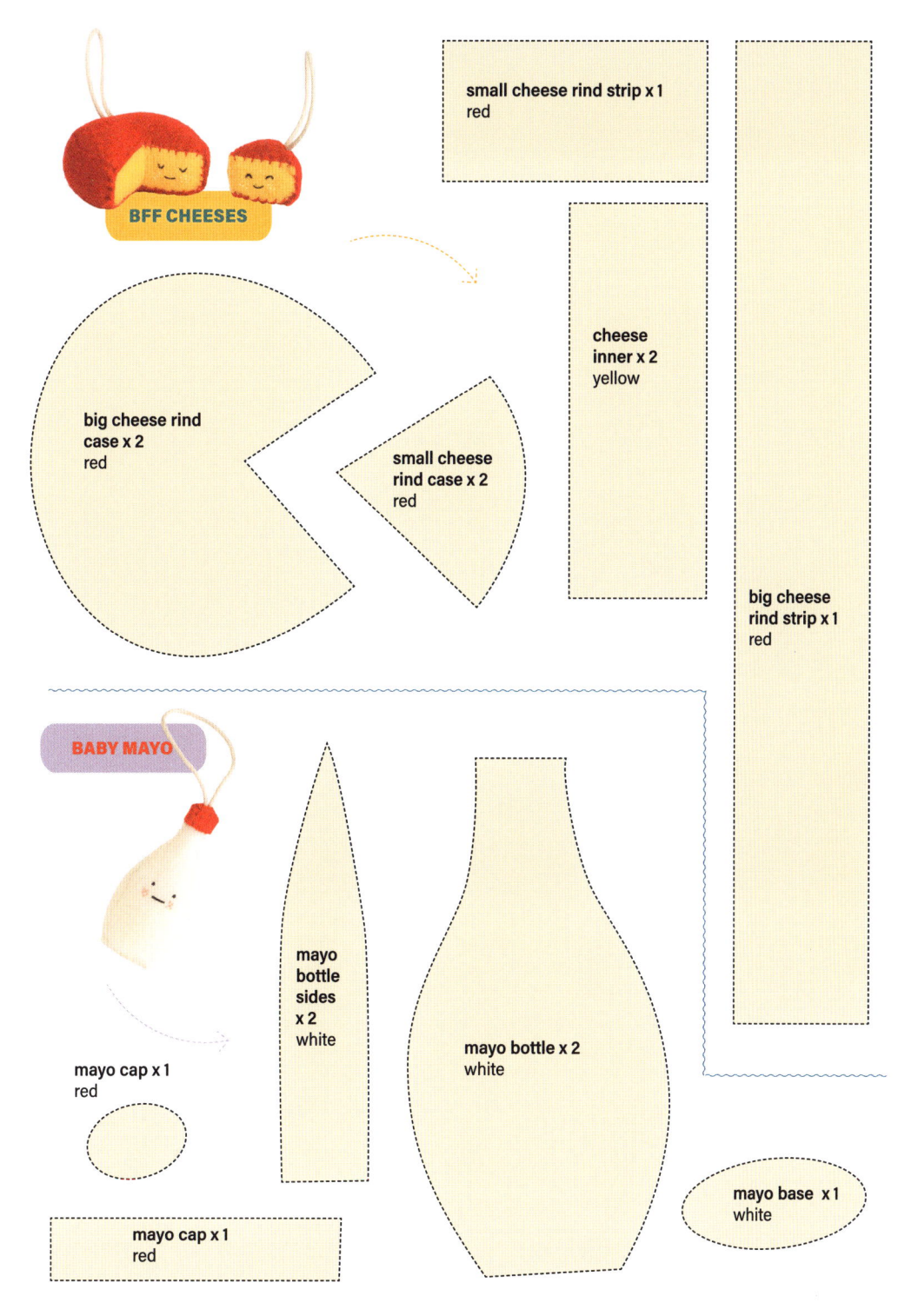

BFF CHEESES

small cheese rind strip x 1
red

cheese
inner x 2
yellow

big cheese rind
case x 2
red

small cheese
rind case x 2
red

big cheese
rind strip x 1
red

BABY MAYO

mayo
bottle
sides
x 2
white

mayo bottle x 2
white

mayo cap x 1
red

mayo base x 1
white

mayo cap x 1
red

FRUIT BOWL

PEACH PAL

peach stone x 1
brown

outer peach x 1
light peach or pink

inner peach x 1
light orange

peach leaf x 1
green

inner apple x 1
white

apple skin x 1
red

apple leaf x 1
green

apple stalk x 1
brown

ALOOF APPLE

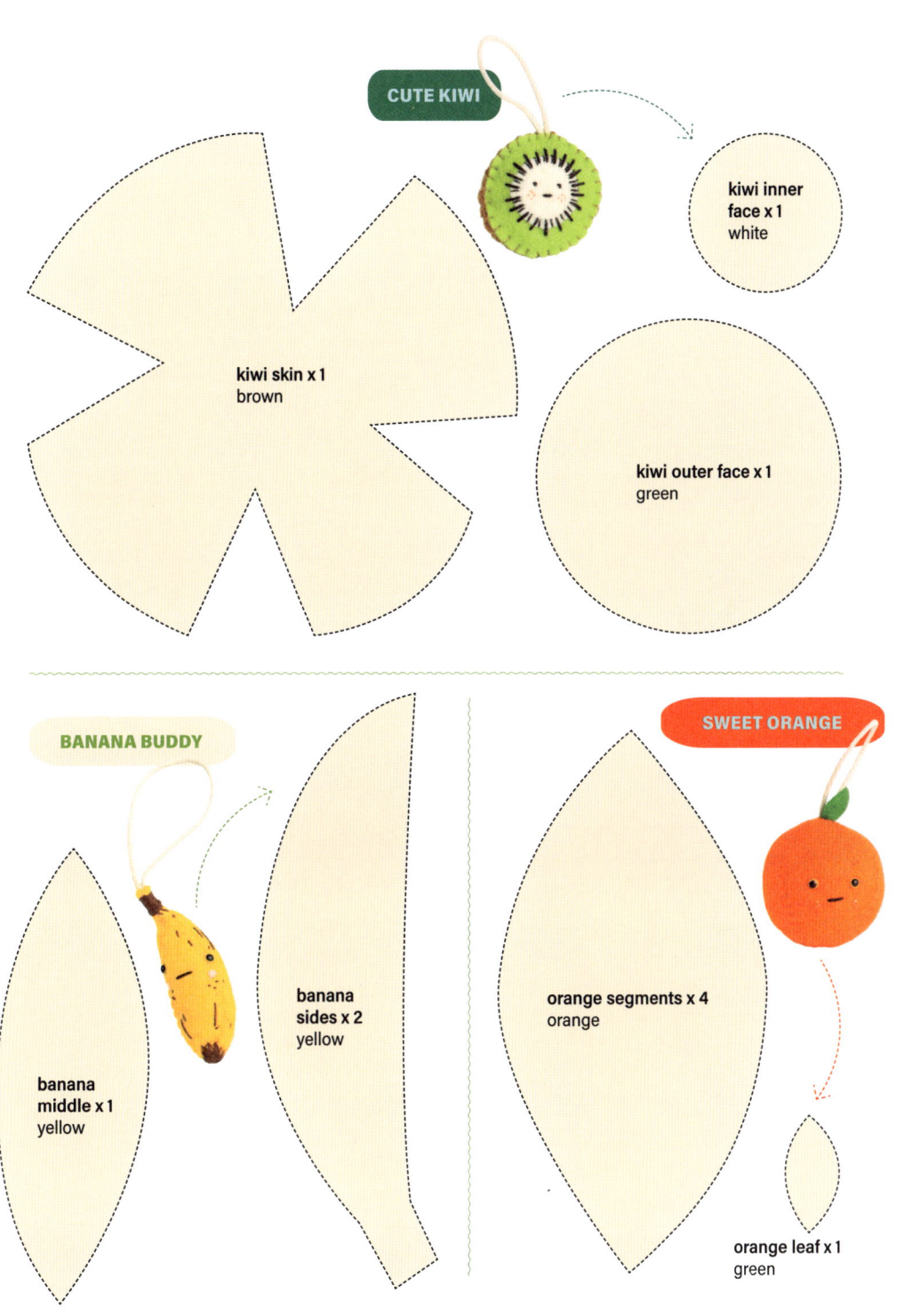

CUTE KIWI

kiwi skin x 1
brown

kiwi inner
face x 1
white

kiwi outer face x 1
green

BANANA BUDDY

SWEET ORANGE

banana
sides x 2
yellow

orange segments x 4
orange

banana
middle x 1
yellow

orange leaf x 1
green

EGGS THREE WAYS

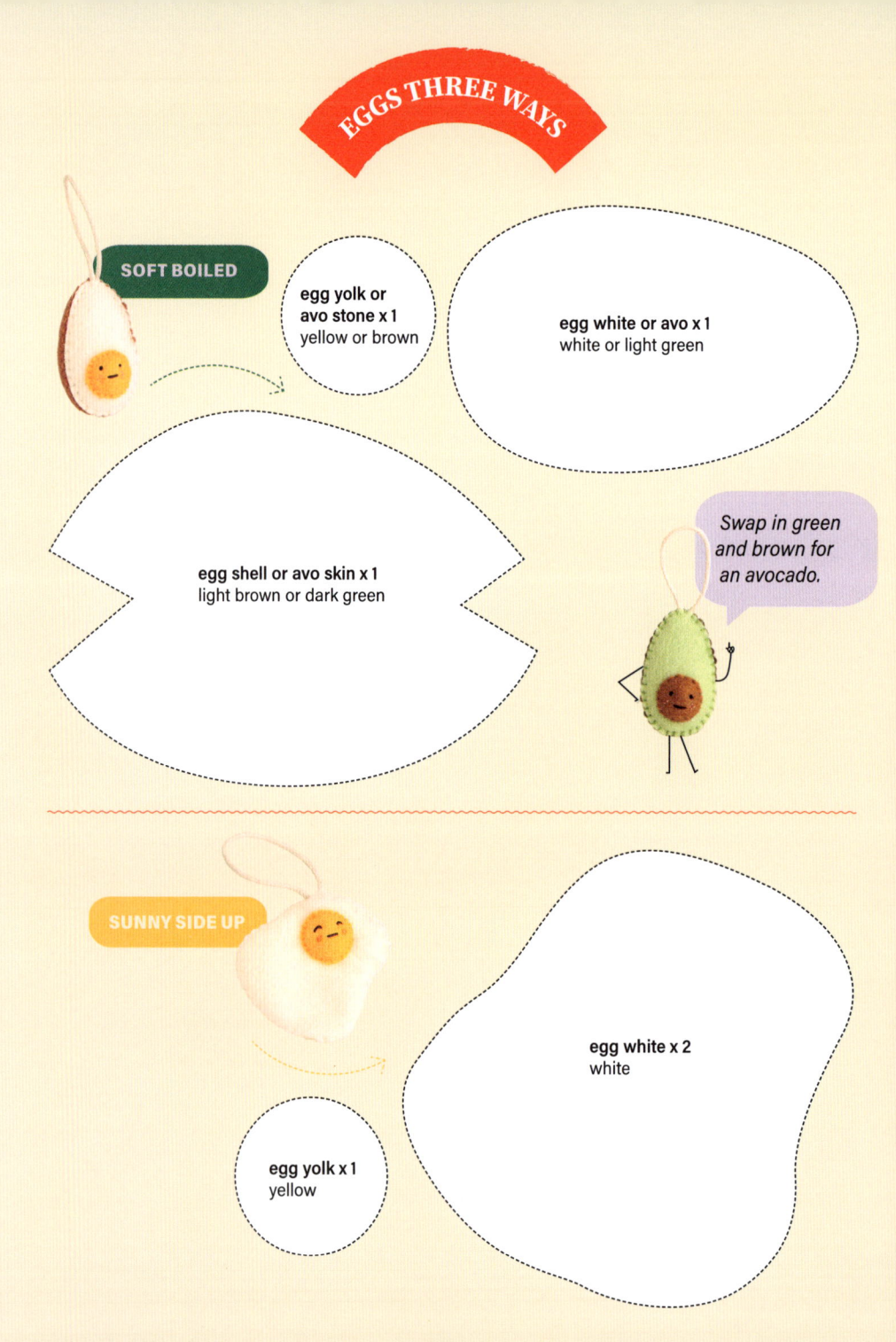

SOFT BOILED

egg yolk or avo stone x 1
yellow or brown

egg white or avo x 1
white or light green

egg shell or avo skin x 1
light brown or dark green

Swap in green and brown for an avocado.

SUNNY SIDE UP

egg white x 2
white

egg yolk x 1
yellow

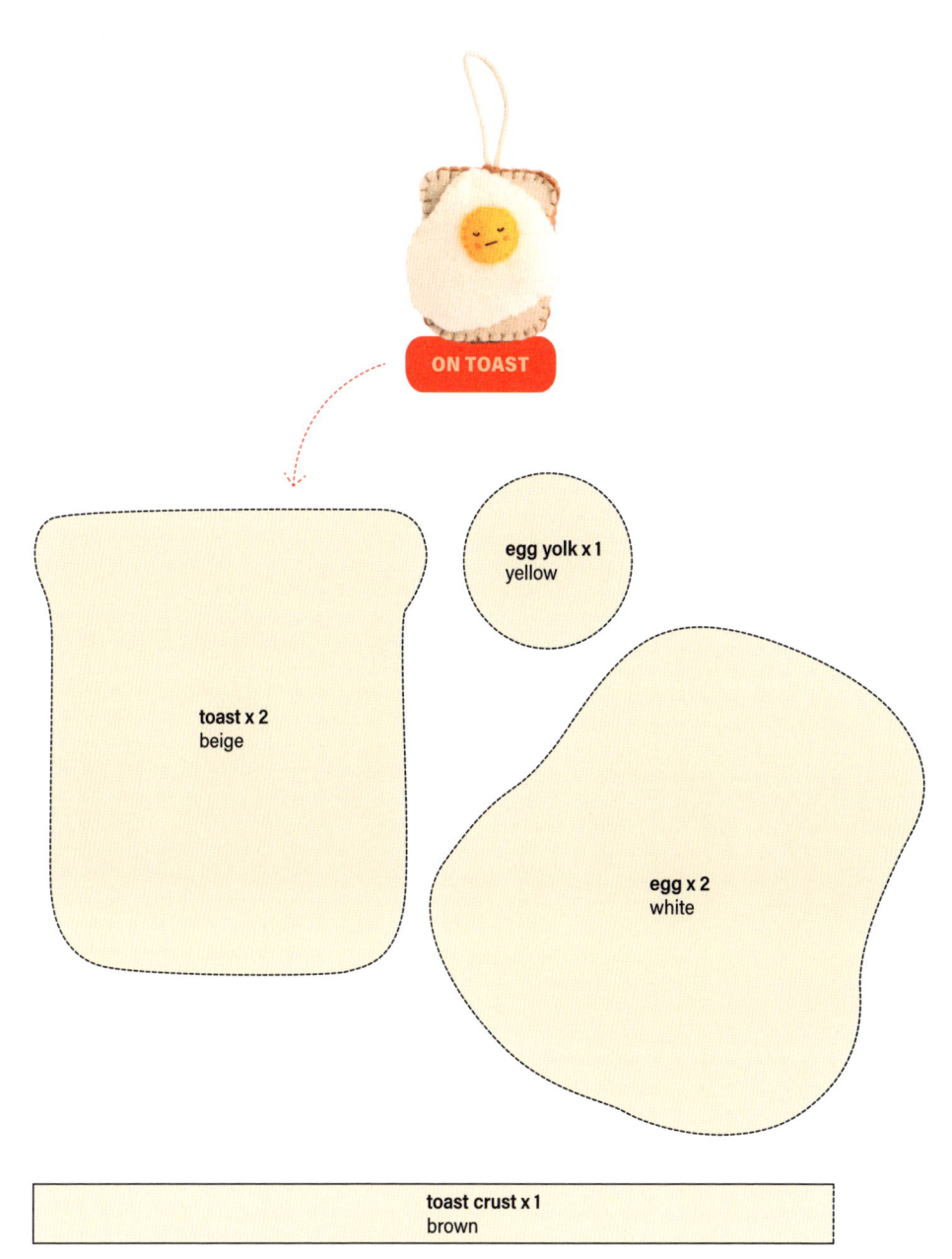

ON TOAST

egg yolk x 1
yellow

toast x 2
beige

egg x 2
white

toast crust x 1
brown

Note: this is a long strip — too long for this book! Trace double the length of this piece to create a crust that is 22.5cm (8 ¾ inches) total length.

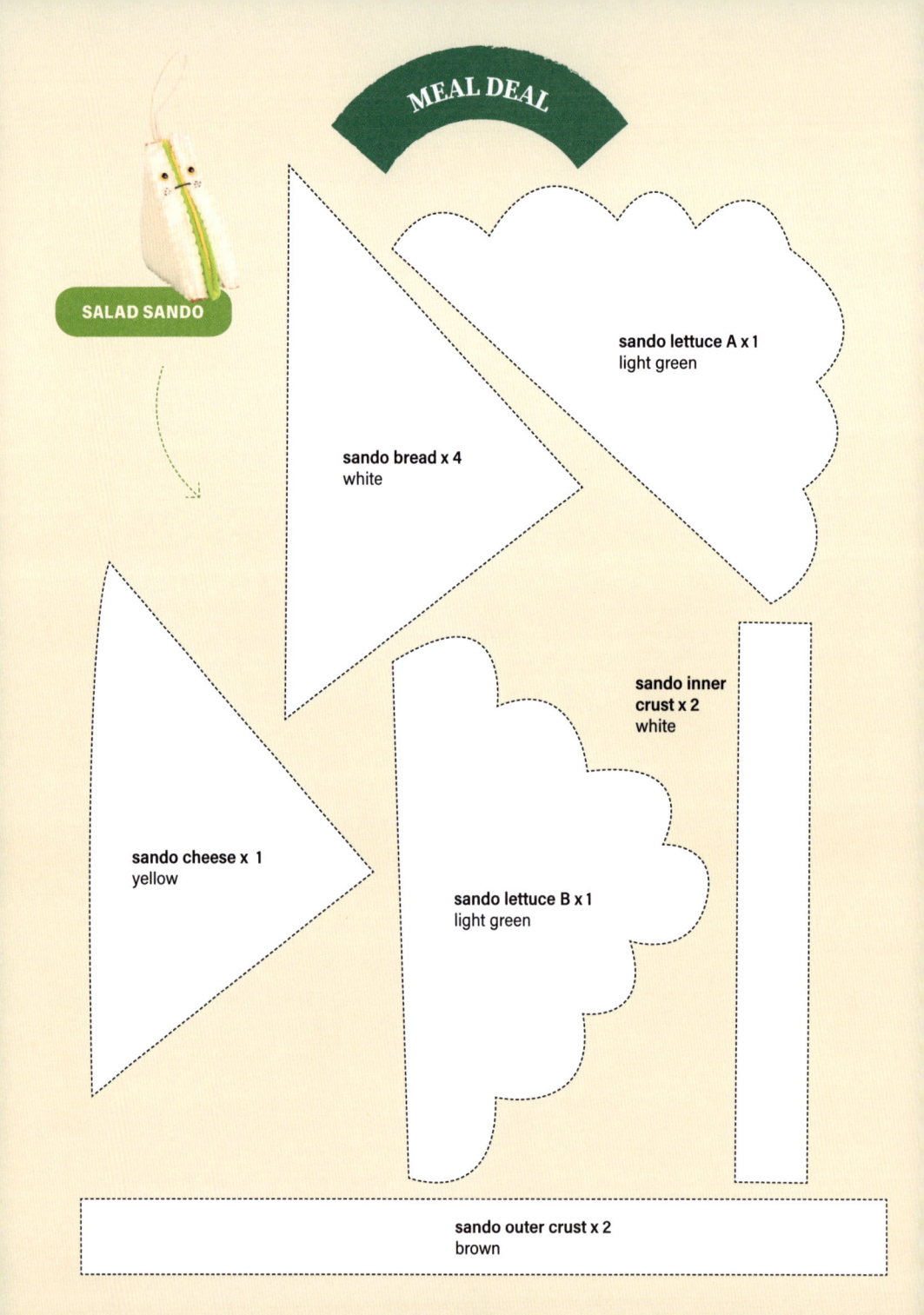

MEAL DEAL

SALAD SANDO

sando lettuce A x 1
light green

sando bread x 4
white

sando inner crust x 2
white

sando cheese x 1
yellow

sando lettuce B x 1
light green

sando outer crust x 2
brown

PACKET O' CRISPS

crisp packet x 2
blue

crisp label x 1
green

tiny potato x 1
light brown

crisp packet edges x 2
green

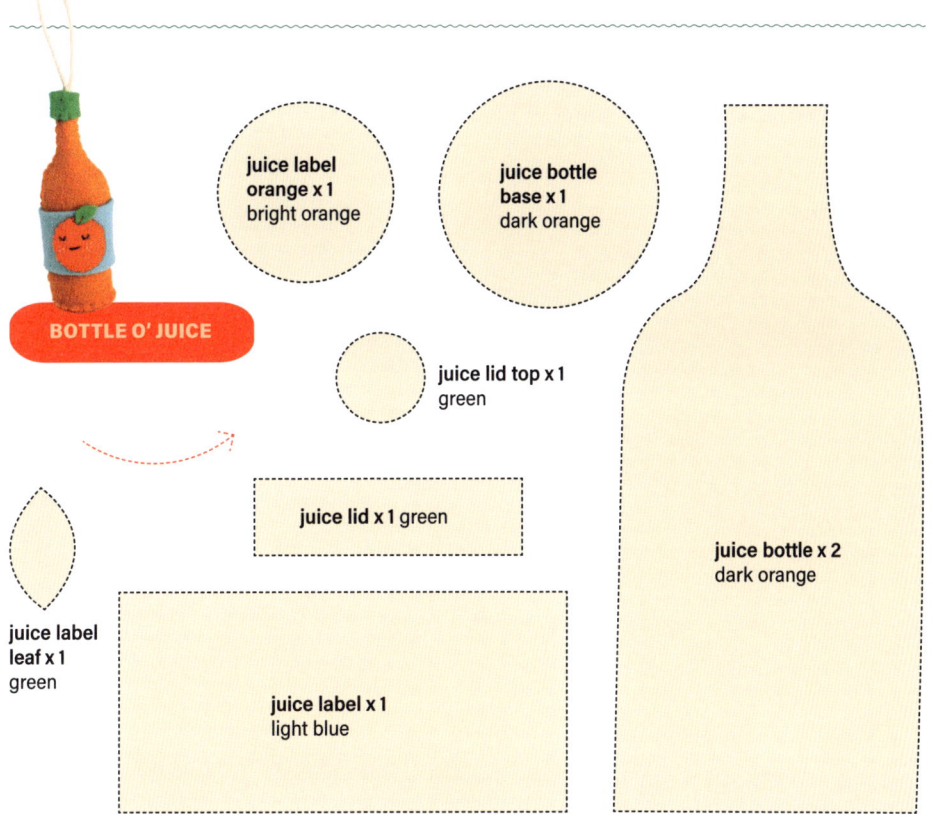

BOTTLE O' JUICE

juice label orange x 1
bright orange

juice bottle base x 1
dark orange

juice lid top x 1
green

juice lid x 1 green

juice label leaf x 1
green

juice label x 1
light blue

juice bottle x 2
dark orange

A DAY AT THE FAIR

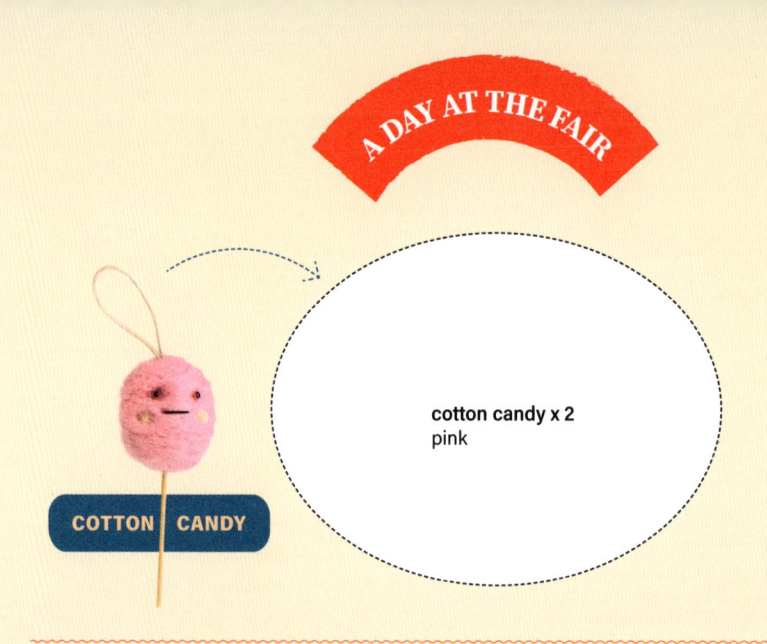

COTTON CANDY

cotton candy x 2
pink

HOT DONUT

donut bag x 2
white

donut x 2
brown

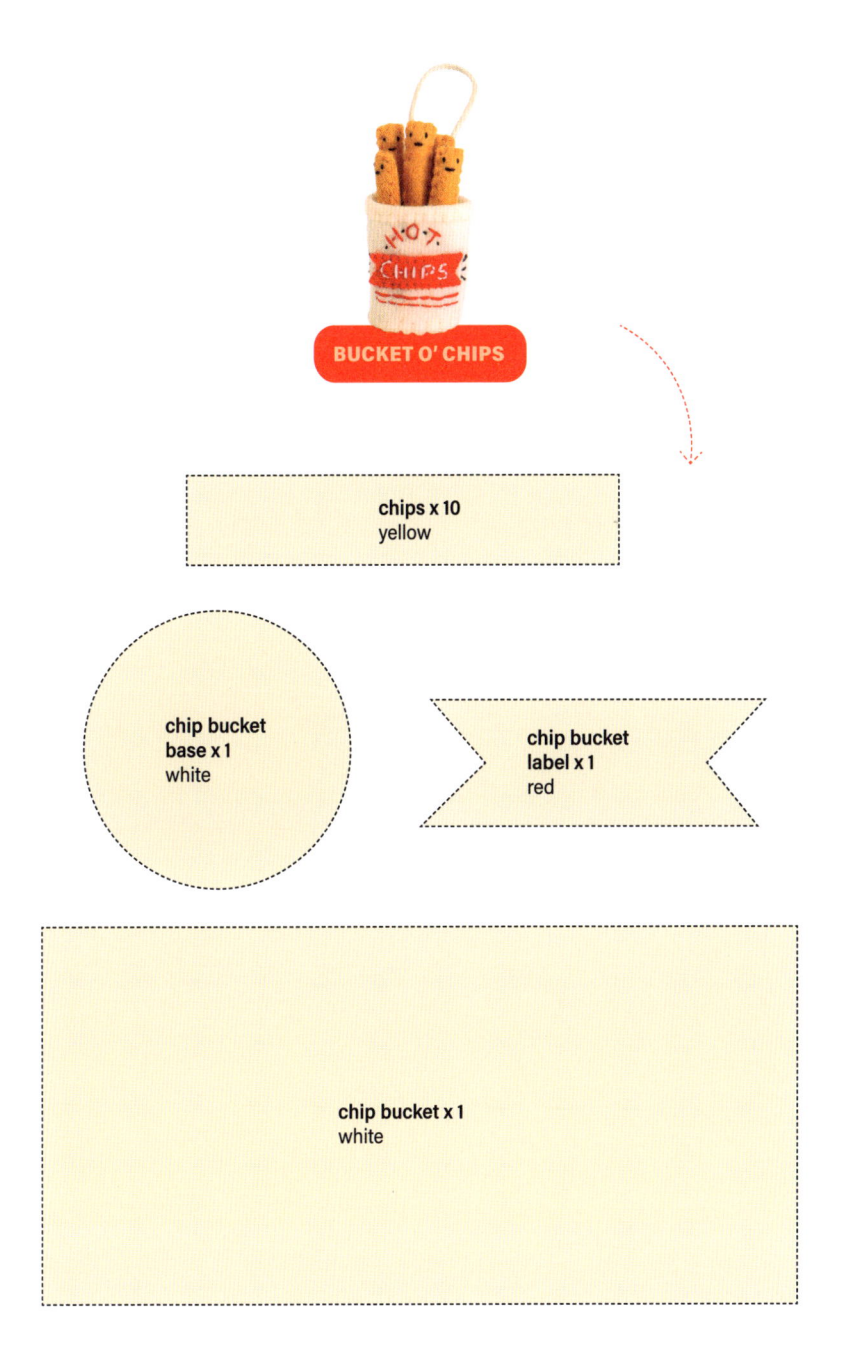

BUCKET O' CHIPS

chips x 10
yellow

chip bucket base x 1
white

chip bucket label x 1
red

chip bucket x 1
white

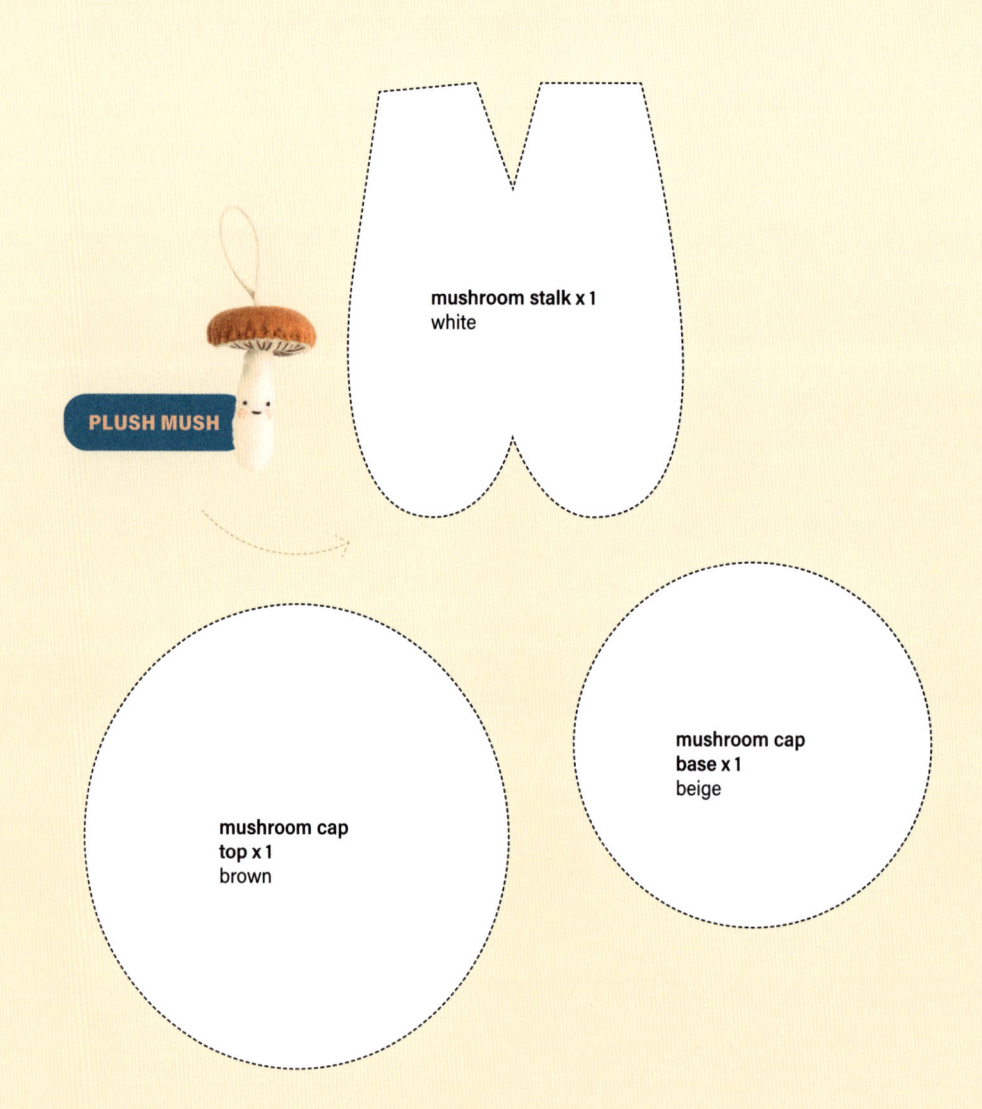

PLUSH MUSH

mushroom stalk x 1
white

**mushroom cap
top x 1**
brown

**mushroom cap
base x 1**
beige

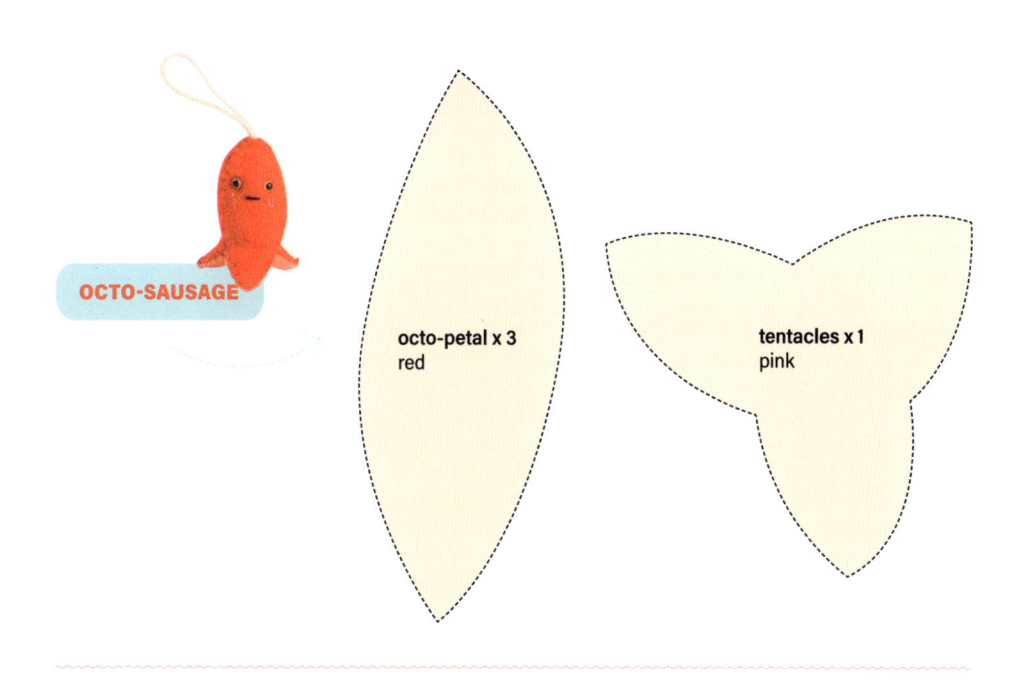

OCTO-SAUSAGE

octo-petal x 3
red

tentacles x 1
pink

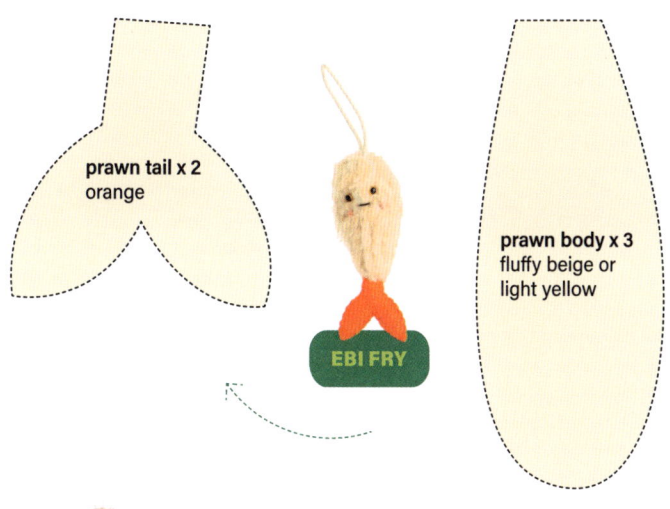

prawn tail x 2
orange

EBI FRY

prawn body x 3
fluffy beige or
light yellow

Thank you to all my pattern testers for their advice and contributions: Abby, Anica, Anna, Catherine, Celeste, Christina, Esther, Helen and Madeline.

Published in 2025 by Smith Street Books
Naarm | Melbourne | Australia
smithstreetbooks.com

Distributed outside of ANZ, North & Latin America by
Thames & Hudson Ltd., 6–24 Britannia Street, London, WC1X 9JD
thamesandhudson.com

EU Authorized Representative: Interart S.A.R.L.
19 rue Charles Auray, 93500 Pantin, Paris, France
productsafety@thameshudson.co.uk; www.interart.fr

ISBN: 978-1-9232-3916-6

Smith Street Books respectfully acknowledges the Wurundjeri
People of the Kulin Nation, who are the Traditional Owners
of the land on which we work, and we pay our respects
to their Elders past and present.

Publisher: Paul McNally
Editor: Lucy Grant
Design, layout and cover art direction: Michelle Mackintosh
Proofreaders: Sophie Dougall and Lucy Heaver

Printed & bound in China by C&C Offset Printing Co., Ltd.

Book 398
10 9 8 7 6 5 4 3 2 1

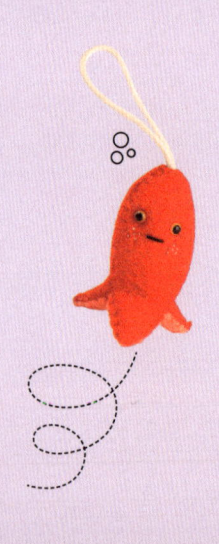

MIX
Paper | Supporting
responsible forestry
FSC® C008047
FSC
www.fsc.org